★
THE
BIG
TIME

JENNIFER LAWRENCE

VALERIE BODDEN

CREATIVE 🍎 EDUCATION

JENNIFER LAWRENCE

TABLE OF CONTENTS

MEET JENNIFER

Jennifer pulls back the string on her bow. She shoots an arrow. Then she hides behind a tree. She does not look at the cameras all around her. But the cameras keep filming. Soon Jennifer's performance will be seen by people around the world.

Jennifer Lawrence is a movie actress. She has starred in hit movies such as *The Hunger Games*. Many people think she is one of the best young actresses today.

....

Jennifer traveled to cities around the world for showings of The Hunger Games

JENNIFER'S CHILDHOOD

Jennifer was born August 15, 1990, in Louisville, Kentucky. She lived with her parents and two older brothers. Jennifer did not like going to school. She did not feel smart.

Jennifer now has fans all across the country

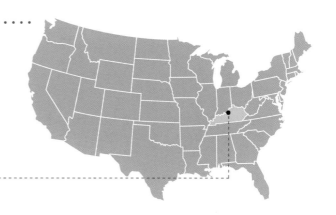

LOUISVILLE, KENTUCKY

GETTING INTO ACTING

Jennifer played field hockey and softball. She was a cheerleader and model, too. But she did not love these activities. She loved acting. Her first roles were in church plays.

....

Jennifer knows how to pose for pictures, thanks to her modeling background

When Jennifer was 14 years old, she went to New York City with her mother. She wanted to find work modeling or acting. She got parts in television commercials and programs. Jennifer finished high school two years early. Then she became a full-time actress.

Jennifer won an award for her early TV work

THE BIG TIME

Soon, Jennifer and her family moved to Los Angeles, California. Jennifer got a part in a TV *sitcom*. She was in more movies, too. In 2010, she acted in *Winter's Bone*. In 2011, she played Mystique in *X-Men: First Class*.

Jennifer repeated her role as Mystique in 2014's X-Men: Days of Future Past

In 2012, Jennifer got the lead role in the movie *The Hunger Games*. The movie was a huge hit. Jennifer has been ***nominated*** for and won many awards. In 2013, she was the second-youngest actress to ever win an ***Academy Award*** for Best Actress.

. . . .

Jennifer played the part of Katniss Everdeen in The Hunger Games

OFF THE SCREEN

When she is not making movies, Jennifer likes to play the guitar. She supports a **charity** for **foster children**. She has made short films for the charity.

Jennifer keeps in shape and enjoys music in her free time

WHAT IS NEXT?

Jennifer planned to star in **sequels** to *The Hunger Games*. She had many other movies planned, too. Jennifer's movies will keep her fans going to the theater for years to come!

The Hunger Games *is the first in a trilogy, or group of three stories*

WHAT JENNIFER SAYS ABOUT ...

FAILURE

"I never considered that I wouldn't be successful.... The phrase 'if it doesn't work out' never popped into my mind."

FRIENDS

"I hang out with the people I always do. Outside of my work life, nothing changes."

MAKING MOVIES

"Moviemaking is really fun.... You have to not take life too seriously [because] at the end of the day you're just making movies and having a great time."

GLOSSARY

Academy Award the most famous kind of award given for movie acting and making movies

charity a group that works to help other people

foster children kids who live temporarily with people who are not their birth family

nominated named as one of the people who could be chosen to win an award

sequels movies that continue the story of an earlier movie

sitcom a funny television show

READ MORE

Gosman, Gillian. *Jennifer Lawrence*. New York: Powerkids, 2012.

Tieck, Sarah. *Jennifer Lawrence: Star of* The Hunger Games. Minneapolis: Abdo, 2013.

WEBSITES

Jennifer Lawrence
http://jenniferslawrence.com/
This is Jennifer's official website, with pictures and videos.

Jennifer Lawrence Biography
http://www.people.com/people/Jennifer_lawrence/
This site has information about Jennifer's life and many pictures, too.

INDEX

PUBLISHED BY Creative Education
P.O. Box 227, Mankato, Minnesota 56002
Creative Education is an imprint of The Creative Company
www.thecreativecompany.us

DESIGN AND PRODUCTION BY Christine Vanderbeek
ART DIRECTION BY Rita Marshall
PRINTED IN the United States of America

PHOTOGRAPHS BY Alamy (Moviestore collection Ltd, Photos 12, Pictorial Press Ltd, ZUMA Press, Inc.), Getty Images (Fotonoticias/FilmMagic, Jeff Vespa/WireImage), iStockphoto (Pingebat, Cole Vineyard), Newscom (Pedro Andrade/PacificCoastNews, VERY FUNNY PRODUCTIONS/Album), Shutterstock (Helga Esteb, Featureflash, MillaF, vipflash)

LIBRARY OF CONGRESS CATALOGING-IN-PUBLICATION DATA
Bodden, Valerie.
Jennifer Lawrence / Valerie Bodden.
p. cm. — (The big time)
Includes index.
Summary: An elementary introduction to the life, work, and popularity of Jennifer Lawrence, an American actress known for her roles in such hit movies as *Winter's Bone* and *The Hunger Games*.

ISBN 978-1-60818-477-4
1. Lawrence, Jennifer, 1990– —Juvenile literature. 2. Actors—United States—Biography—Juvenile literature. I. Title.
PN2287.L28948B63 2013
791.4302'8092—dc23 [B]   2013014553

FIRST EDITION
9 8 7 6 5 4 3 2 1